THE POWER OF PRAYER

A Science Educator's Experience

[handwritten inscription: To: Helen & Gary, Very Best Wishes, Dana M. Barry]

Dana M. Barry, Ph.D.

Strategic Book Publishing

Strategic Book Publishing
An imprint of Strategic Book Group
P.O. Box 333
Durham, CT 06422
www.StrategicBookGroup.com

ISBN: 978-1-60860-748-8

Printed in the United States of America

Book Design: Judy Maenle

DEDICATION

*This book is for everyone
on the journey of life.*

ACKNOWLEDGEMENT

I thank God, the Blessed Mother, my parents (Daniel and Celia Malloy), my family (especially my husband James and my four sons James, Brian, Daniel, and Eric), my colleagues (especially Dr. Roger Haw of Malaysia and Dr. Hideyuki Kanematsu of Japan), my friends, and Strategic Book Publishing, for their inspiration and continued support.

TABLE OF CONTENTS

INTRODUCTION

I believe that prayers are powerful and can be used to promote world peace and to unite our global community. People of various religions throughout the world pray. They value the power of prayers. As a known author and science educator, I have had opportunities to visit Malaysia and Japan where I witnessed Muslims and Buddhists in deep meditative thought and prayer. Also, I have had discussions with members of these religious groups, where they shared their thoughts and beliefs with me. It is true that individuals worldwide have similar needs and dreams. We are all really praying for the same things such as world peace, good health, prosperity, a successful life, and an adequate supply of food and water. In my heart, I believe that humans are from God and have much good within them. Most individuals (whom I have met throughout the world) are kind, caring, and thoughtful. Life on Earth could be more like Heaven if each individual, especially our global leaders, would pray for this goal and treat others with kindness and respect.

I have had exceptional religious experiences for over thirty years because of powerful prayers (praying with deep concentration and faith). I believe that God wants me to share these unique and meaningful events, so that others may benefit and recognize the special plans that God has for them.

I was motivated to write this book by a Christmas gift that I received from my husband in 2008. It was a text about science and religion. As soon as I started to read it, I had an inner feeling that it was time for my religious experiences to be shared with others. Since I strongly believe in the power of prayer, I said many prayers and asked God for guidance in writing *The Power of Prayer: A Science Educator's Experience.*

This book conveys a special message to the reader. God has helped people for centuries and continues to do so. We only need to ask Him. Since we live in a troubled world filled with many challenging problems, it is a good time to seek God's assistance. He is always there and ready to help all of us: the poor, the rich, religious leaders, lay people, and all of those living in large cities, small towns, and various countries throughout the world.

CHAPTER 1

The Beginning

My Request

Thirty years ago, I was very disappointed with life. Nothing seemed to work out the way I wanted it to. My father was sick with cancer. I prayed for him, but he suffered and died anyway. I endured pain from the misfortunes of close friends. Also, many career opportunities passed me by. Feeling sad and unhappy, I put my faith on the line. In a special prayer, I told God that my religious beliefs were sitting on the fence. I requested a special sign to help maintain and strengthen my faith.

Growing Up

I am the oldest of six children and grew up in Clinton, a central New York town, where Hamilton College is located. Having been brought up Catholic, I received the sacraments, said prayers at meals and before going to bed, and went to church, regularly. Also I attended parochial schools during my elementary education. As a second grader, I went to St. Michael's School in Warsaw, New York, and had an opportunity to spend a day at the convent with my teacher, Sister Asenta. She was very nice and volunteered to watch me because my parents had to be out of town for some reason. I can still picture her smiling face, as she gave me a guided tour and introduced me to the other nuns.

While growing up I always believed in God, but never thought deeply or seriously about my religion. In part this may be a result of my busy lifestyle. Being the oldest child meant that I had many duties at home. I washed dishes, helped with the cooking and laundry, and watched my younger brothers. One of them even called me mommy.

The first year of high school was the most challenging and yet the most eventful for me. I received my highest grades, some prestigious awards, and even won a speed skating trophy when I was only fourteen years old. I felt very happy and proud. However, I also have some sad memories from that year. During the winter, my mother became so upset upon hearing the news of her mother's death that she fell on the sidewalk and broke her leg. My mother, Celia, actually had three breaks in her leg and had to wear a cast up to her hip for many months. She spent much of that time in a wheelchair. This made it almost impossible for her to care for my three-year-old brother Eric and my one-year-old brother Gary. Celia had some hired help for several hours each day. However my father Daniel, my sister Karen (who is one year younger than I am), and I did most everything that needed to be done during her recovery period. In addition to household duties, I had part-time jobs like babysitting and was involved in sports and music organizations. I continued this lifestyle (of working, studying, and taking part in extracurricular activities), as I pursued undergraduate degrees in chemistry and science education.

CHAPTER 2

Spiritual Awakening

The Sign

In 1971, after graduating from college, I got married. I worked in industry for awhile and pursued graduate degrees in chemistry and science education. Then my first child James Daniel was born in 1975. Next my second son Brian Patrick was born in 1976. Later my third son Daniel Thomas was born in 1978, and my fourth son Eric Michael was born in 1979. During this time period I had several part-time evening jobs and played trumpet in a band, but basically stayed home for several years to take care of my children. I was not constantly on the run, so I had some time to pray and think about God as well as life in general. In 1978 my father was diagnosed with cancer, while I was pregnant with my son Daniel who is named after him. It is interesting to note that my father died in May and seemed to be replaced by my son who was born in May. I was very close to my father and said many prayers for his recovery, but he died anyway. I also prayed for other sick people and for special things that I wanted in life. It seemed like none of my prayers were being answered, so I was not happy.

As a result of what I considered to be disappointing answers to my prayers, I became a doubting Thomas (like the disciple). Thomas needed solid proof to believe that Jesus had risen from the dead. He told the other disciples who had seen Jesus, "I will never believe it without probing the nail prints in his hands, without putting my finger in the nail marks, and my hand into his side" (John 20:25).[1] Days later Thomas became a believer, because he saw Jesus appear to the disciples while he was with them (John 20:26-29).

I privately communicated my feelings with God in Prayer and asked for a sign to strengthen my faith. I prayed many rosaries for months asking God to grant my request.

Then one day to my surprise, strange things started to happen. While my husband Jim was at work and I was home with our sons aged four, three, one, and a newborn, I sensed a mysterious presence though I saw nothing. It was a feeling like someone was looking over your shoulder or had quickly walked behind you. It continued for several weeks. Each day I would carefully and conscientiously enter the rooms of my house. Then something more strange happened. The event took place in the bedroom when my husband and I retired for the night. A tapping sound resembling the Morse code was played on our metal bedposts. It sounded like a metal spoon being tapped on a glass. At first I thought my husband was tapping his wedding ring on the bedpost and he thought I was tapping my ring on the bedpost. Then one night, when we both had our hands in front of us, we discovered that the sound was being made by a mysterious presence. This was frightening at first, but we soon

---

1. All Bible references in this book are from *The New American Bible* (The New Catholic Translation); Catholic Publishers, Inc.: New York, 1971.

got accustomed to this occurrence, which took place nightly for several weeks.

Finally one evening in late October at about 11:30 p.m., during the last week of hearing the tapping sounds, I encountered a spirit in our kitchen. My husband and four sons were already asleep. I was standing in the narrow hallway (outside of my bedroom) which led to an open kitchen. A wall phone was about twenty feet in front of me (in the kitchen) at the other end of the hall. I was preparing to turn the lights out for the night, when to my amazement a spirit seeming to come from nowhere appeared at the wall phone. I froze in place and didn't move. I was in a state of shock. The spirit had its back to me, while standing next to the telephone, as if it were making a call. It had a human shape but was transparent and seemed to be gracefully bouncing up and down several inches above the floor. Suddenly the apparition turned around and faced me. Its head looked like the yellow Sun and had slits for eyes and a mouth. No hands and no feet were visible. The body appeared sky blue in color and was lit up. This spirit, which seemed to be made of light, bounced quietly down the hall within five feet of me and stared for a moment. Then it disappeared as rapidly as it had appeared. I immediately prayed to God saying that I was very grateful for the sign, but never wanted to see a spirit again. I also asked God to forgive me for my doubting faith.

The next day I discussed the spiritual encounter with my husband and also decided to share it with several priests. Priests told me that the blue and yellow are heavenly colors so that my prayers had been answered. It was at this time, that I promised God I would say a rosary every day until I die. So far I have said the equivalent of

Apparition with the Sun for a Head

(Sketch by Dana Barry)

one rosary per day for thirty years. My rosaries are for everyone (the sick, the poor, those suffering in any way, the priests, etc.) and for all souls. I also pray for world peace and sometimes devote one or more rosaries for someone in special need of prayers.

Spiritual awakening can happen to anyone at any time in any place. St. Nicholas of Flue was a religious person who led a diverse life. In 1467 Nikolaus was a prosperous landowner and local official in Switzerland, who lived with his wife and nine children. By the age of 50, he had raised his family and reflected on his full and happy life. However, he was troubled by a deep inner religious feeling. He began to pray devotedly asking to be brought closer to God. His prayers were answered by a visit from the Blessed Trinity and additional visions. As a result, he left his family and earthly possessions to live his final 20 years as the holy hermit called Brother Klaus (1).

Mother Teresa said, "Yesterday is gone. Tomorrow has not yet come. We have only today. Let us begin . . ." (2).

CHAPTER 3
The Rosary

Rosary Meaning

The rosary is both a string of beads with a crucifix and a set of prayers and meditations. Its name comes from the Latin "rosarium," which means a crown of roses. The beads represent prayers and help one keep track of the number said. They are grouped into five sets of ten, with a special bead separating each set. At the end of the last decade is a picture of the Blessed Mother. Below Her is a bead separating a small chain of three beads followed by another separate bead. The rosary culminates with the crucifix.

The main prayers of the rosary are the Lord's Prayer (represented by the beads separating each decade), the Hail Mary (which is said for each bead of the decade), and the Glory Be to the Father (which is recited at the end of each set of ten Hail Mary's). While praying each decade, one meditates on a particular Mystery of the Rosary. These Mysteries are events in the lives of Jesus Christ and his Mother, the Blessed Virgin Mary. Each meditation is determined by the time of year and the day of the week. The traditional fifteen Mysteries of the Rosary were finalized by the 16th Century. They include The Joyful Mysteries, The Sorrowful Mysteries, and The

Glorious Mysteries. The Luminous Mysteries (the new optional ones) were announced by Pope John Paul II in 2002.

The twenty Mysteries of the Rosary and their Bible listings are provided.

The Joyful Mysteries
The Annunciation of Gabriel to Mary (Luke 1:26-38)
The Visitation of Mary to Elizabeth (Luke 1:39-56)
The Birth of Our Lord (Luke 2:1-21)
The Presentation of Our Lord (Luke 2:22-38)
The Finding of Our Lord in the Temple (Luke 2:41-52)

The Sorrowful Mysteries
The Agony of Our Lord in the Garden
    (Matthew 26:36-56)
Our Lord is Scourged at the Pillar (Matthew 27:26)
Our Lord is Crowned with Thorns (Matthew 27:29)
Our Lord Carries the Cross (Matthew 27:32)
The Death of Our Lord (Matthew 27:45-50)

The Glorious Mysteries
The Resurrection of Our Lord (John 20:1-29)
The Ascension of Our Lord into Heaven
    (Luke 24:50-51)
The Descent of the Holy Spirit (Acts 2:1-41)
The Assumption of Mary into Heaven
The Coronation of Mary (Revelation 12:1)

The Luminous Mysteries
The Baptism of Our Lord (Matthew 3:13-16)
The Wedding at Cana (John 2:1-11)

The Proclamation of the Kingdom of God
   (Mark 1:14-15)
The Transfiguration of Our Lord (Matthew 17:1-8)
The Last Supper (Matthew 26:17-30)

Rosary Power

St. Louis De Montfort was a strong advocate of the rosary who said, "There is no limit to the power of the rosary . . ." (3).

In October 1571, Europe faced a hopeless battle against the Turks. The Turks had conquered the Middle East and went on to take control of the seafaring islands of Crete and Cyprus. They threatened Sicily, Venice, and even Rome. Pope Pius V Ghislieri called upon the Christians of Europe to form a league of defense. Since he was devoted to Our Lady, he also asked them to pray the rosary.

On the first Sunday of October, the Christian ships were surrounded by the Turks off the coast of Greece. However they were able to break through and by the end of the day most of the Turks either retreated or drowned. Pope Pius was so very grateful to Our Lady for the victory, that he ordered an annual commemoration in Her honor (4). Currently October is the month of the rosary, and October 7th is the special day to honor Our Lady of the Rosary.

CHAPTER 4

Prayers Answered

New Home

My prayers to God for a sign were answered in such an extraordinary way that I promised to say a rosary each day until I die. During the twenty years that followed, I have said thousands of rosaries and have had prayers answered in God's way, which is the best way. Some examples are provided.

In 1989, after living at the same residence in Canton for over 15 years, we decided to buy a better house. We had been house-shopping for several months and finally found the answer to our dream. My husband and I and our four sons fell in love with a large, old, one-story house that was for sale on Howe Boulevard in Canton. It had a nice yard, an extended two car garage, five large bedrooms, an intercom system, and most importantly a beautiful pool that was 20 feet wide and 40 feet long. We placed a bid on this expensive house, which was really out of our price range. The owner, who was actually selling the house without assistance from a Realtor, informed us that several other people were also bidding on the house. It soon came to our attention that all the interested parties loved the place just as much as we did. Therefore we decided to pray so that hopefully this house would be ours. Several months of patient waiting went by before we found out the final outcome of this house. To our great disappointment, the house was not sold to any of the bidders, but instead given to the Methodist Church for a modest price. To say the least, our whole family was heartbroken. However, we decided to keep a positive attitude and continued to look for another home. To our great surprise we found a nice, newer, cheaper home, with the same size swimming pool (that our dream house had). We quickly bought this house and are still living there today. God truly answered our prayers in the best way. The older home that we originally wanted was very expensive and needed to be painted and repaired. Also the swimming pool had major problems that we were not aware of during the bidding process. We believe that God helped us to save money and buy the better house.

Eric's Accident

During this same time period, my faculty position of two years at Potsdam College ended. My job involved teaching elementary and secondary science methods as well as supervising student teachers. I enjoyed the work but knew in advance that it would be a short-term position. I prayed for another employment opportunity to arise. However, I soon found out that God had something more important for me to do.

It was another typical hockey weekend for our family. I served as the coach of a house league team that included the Barry line. James and Brian usually played defense positions, while Daniel and Eric Barry were forwards. It was a thrill to have my four sons play hockey together. Canton had several different house league teams, each with its own local sponsor. The teams practiced and competed in games several times a week during the winter season.

On this particular weekend, my youngest son Eric informed me that he had been invited to a special overnight party. He really wanted to go, even if it meant missing his early Saturday morning game. I insisted that he go to hockey, but he reminded me that he was ten years old and never had a chance to stay overnight at a friend's house. So my husband and I finally agreed to let Eric spend the night with his friend. I do not have extrasensory perception, but during that Friday afternoon I had an awful feeling that something was wrong. It was such an intense emotion that I asked Eric to put on his holy medals before he left the house. This sad, persistent feeling remained with me throughout that day and evening. I kept silently telling myself to ignore it and that Eric would be okay.

At 2:00 a.m., my husband and I were startled by a ringing telephone. My husband mechanically got out of bed, answered the phone, and then crawled back under the covers. I still had that awful feeling in my gut, so I quickly asked him who called. He was half asleep, but said it was something about Eric. I immediately ran to the phone and called the residence where Eric was spending the night. As soon as a voice answered, I frantically asked if Eric was okay. The response was, "I don't know but the ambulance has just arrived."

Hysterically I screamed into the phone, "What has happened to my son Eric?"

After a brief pause, a member of the rescue squad replied in a calm but serious voice. "Eric has had a bad accident and cut an artery in his arm. The good news is that we have been able to stop the bleeding. Meet us right away at the emergency room."

I was in a state of shock and felt sick to my stomach, but managed to say "Thanks. We will be there."

Eric was closely examined by the emergency room doctor, who told us that our son needed a neurosurgeon. He said that in addition to his cut artery, Eric also had major damage to the nerves in his wrist and hand. Since we were frantic and highly upset, my husband and I blurted out in unison, "Please hurry and get the best surgeon possible!" The doctor immediately called the Syracuse hospital and made arrangements for Eric's operation. Our great friend Dave Reynolds drove the Barry family to Syracuse, where Eric endured more than seven hours of microsurgery.

Fortunately Eric had an expert neurosurgeon, so the operation was a success. However, the recovery time was long. During that year, I spent lots of time taking Eric to physical therapy sessions and to places where he could exercise, especially since he was not allowed to attend physical education classes at school. His therapist taught me the stretching and strengthening exercises that Eric needed to do and how to massage his arm and wrist to break up the scar tissue. He also told me that the more exercises Eric did, the better his chances of regaining use of his hand and fingers. I took on the duties of my new job (Eric's private physical therapist) with great determination and enthusiasm. Thanks to God, by the end of that year Eric was basically healed and functioning well.

Music Assistance

Some prayers have been answered the way I requested them. In the mid 1980s I served on the faculty at Mater Dei College in Ogdensburg, NY, where I taught health, biology, and other science courses. Since I was a musician, I volunteered to play trumpet with Sister Anne Hogan (a Sister of St. Joseph) for special College functions and activities. I also played trumpet with the organist Ellie Beauvais at my Church, St. Mary's in Canton. On several occasions in both locations, I was expected to play difficult music and fanfares for large audiences. Lacking confidence and feeling very nervous, I asked God to please help me play the trumpet. To my great surprise, the sounds echoing from my horn were truly wonderful. It was as though the notes were being played by someone else.

I have been a member of our Church choir for many years. A few times when I was the only person singing with Mark Darou, a piano player at our Church, we performed songs that I never saw before. Realizing this unfortunate situation at the beginning of Mass, I immediately asked God for help. My prayers were answered in such a way that I anticipated all of the musical sounds correctly.

Other Help

Also I credit my published books, prestigious awards, honors, and unique experiences to God's special way of answering my prayers.

Ever since high school, my dream has been to visit and work with people in other countries. I took lots of

17

French and Latin courses, so that I could major in French at college and eventually travel to France. However during my freshman year, I became less interested in French and more interested in science. When I met my husband Jim in a chemistry laboratory, he convinced me to change my major to chemistry. I was happy with this career change, but realized that it might not provide me with a chance to work in other countries. I continued to pray for this special opportunity. My prayers were answered thirty years later. Don't give up on God. He hears our pleas and prayers and answers them in a time and way that is best.

CHAPTER 5

Foreign Collaborators

Professional Experience

Since the 1980s up to the present time, I have had a variety of jobs. They include my current position as senior technical writer at Clarkson's Center for Advanced Materials Processing, chemical consultant for Corning at their Canton plant, and science educator for the Canton Middle School, Lisbon High School, Mater Dei College, Canton College of Technology, Potsdam College, and Clarkson University. Using my diverse work experiences, I wrote several popular books for teachers and their students, science articles in award-winning journals, a featured paper ("Hazard Communication and Training: A Prototype") published in the *Journal of Environmental Health* (5), and the cover story "Chem-Is-Tree" in the *Journal of Chemical Education* (6). Also while serving as an administrator in Clarkson's Space Grant Program in 1998, I had the honor of organizing the world's first MoonLink and NearLink Space Missions with support from NASA (National Aeronautic and Space Administration) and Space Explorers, Inc. In addition, I carried out the world's first MarsLink Mission in 2000 at Clarkson. As a result of these accomplishments, I received several awards and had my bio information listed in national and international Who's Who type publications.

Dr. Roger Haw

In January of 2000 I was very pleasantly surprised to receive a letter from Malaysia, especially since I didn't know anyone in that Country. Quickly and excitedly I opened the envelope and saw that it was written by Dr. Roger Haw (Haw Boon Hong), Co-Founder of Ansted University. The first sentence read, "Greetings and Congratulations to you for being listed in *The Outstanding People of the 20th Century,* published by the International Biographical Centre in Cambridge, England."

I couldn't believe my eyes. It was truly amazing that a person from the other side of the world had read about me in a book and actually taken the time to personally send me a letter of congratulations. I was immediately impressed with this special individual, Dr. Roger Haw.

Dr. Roger Haw and I continued to communicate throughout the year. Soon I was appointed an Honorary Member of Ansted University's Advisory Board and agreed to help with publications and science-related research and programs. In 2001 Dr. Haw invited me to serve as a Visiting Professor in Malaysia. This appeared to be an opportunity of a lifetime, so I was very happy and honored to accept his offer. For years I had wanted to collaborate with people in other countries. God heard my prayers and answered them in a time and way that was best for me.

During my first visit to Malaysia, I gave presentations about Space Exploration at the National Planetarium in Kuala Lumpur (the capital of Malaysia) and at St.

Xavier's School in Penang. Also I participated in a special graduation ceremony, in which Ansted awarded me an Honorary Doctorate for my excellent contributions to Science Education.

While there, I discovered and enjoyed the beauty of this multi-cultural Country. Its tropical flowers, unique rock formations, waterfalls, and colorful, ornate temples truly thrilled me. Also I found the people to be friendly. They belong to three main groups. Most of them are Malays, who are Muslims. The other two groups include the Chinese, who are mostly Buddhists, and the Indians who are mainly Hindus. The national language is Bahasa Malaysia (Malay) but English is widely spoken.

Since my initial visit, I have been promoted to Scientific Board President for Ansted University and have returned to Malaysia as a Visiting Professor in 2004 and 2007.

My host and current collaborator Dr. Roger Haw is Chinese and lives on Penang Island, one of the most important industrialized states in Malaysia. He is a kind, caring, and brilliant leader. Dr. Haw is founder of the Ansted Service Center located in Malaysia and Co-Founder of Ansted University, British Virgin Islands, United Kingdom. Ansted is a private, open international university, with accomplished faculty members from many countries. A major goal of the University is to promote world peace by cultivating the practice of social responsibility. Social responsibility practice means to carry out projects and activities that benefit society. To help achieve this goal, Dr. Haw created the prestigious award called ASRIA (Ansted Social Responsibility International Award). This coveted award is presented to winning individuals, institutions, and other organizations throughout the world, in recognition of their excellent social responsibility practices. MUCOS Pharma (a company in the Czech Republic that imports and distributes therapy drugs) received the ASRIA award in 2004. This company helps thousands of children in orphanages by providing them with art workshops, training, temporary housing, and assistance in obtaining jobs. We hope to have 20 million participants in Ansted's Social Responsibility Program by 2015.

I feel that it is God's plan for me (in the capacity of Scientific Board President) to support and assist Dr. Roger Haw and Ansted University in their efforts to pursue world peace by promoting the practice of social responsibility.

Dr. Hideyuki Kanematsu

In 2001, my current collaborator from Japan discovered me in cyberspace. This unique way of meeting was truly amazing. It was made possible by a former Clarkson Chemistry Professor, Dr. Don Rosenthal. After retiring, he became a Professor Emeritus and spent lots of time organizing online conferences for the American Chemical Society.

This particular year he was in charge of a special Confchem Conference in Science Education that focused on the Environment. Since Professor Rosenthal already knew about my experiences as a science teacher and writer, I wasn't completely surprised when he asked me for a favor. He needed another paper for this conference. I agreed to contribute one, "The Environmental Risks of Using Combustion as a Source of Energy," and to be available for answering questions about it (7).

The day for discussing my paper arrived. Since it was my turn to answer inquiries, I was comfortably seated in my office staring at the incoming mail screen on the computer. While wondering if anyone took the time to read my paper, several messages appeared. I was thrilled to read them because they came from Japan, one of my favorite countries. Japan, known as the land of the rising sun, mainly consists of the following four islands: Honshu in the center, Hokkaido in the north, and Shikoku and Kyushu to the south. It is mountainous, but includes beautiful cities and temples as well as tea bushes and rice fields. Most of the people are Buddhists. They are very polite and enjoy giving gifts to their guests.

My exciting mail came from Professor Hideyuki Kanematsu of Japan. He was very interested in my paper, which presented the risks of using combustion as a source of energy. It described the greenhouse effect, air pollution, smog, and acid rain. In addition to being informative, my paper encouraged students in grades 7–12 to analyze these risks and to brainstorm for solutions such as alternate energy sources and energy conservation. Student activities and resources for further reading were also provided.

Professor Kanematsu was impressed with my writing style and with the student activities. He told me that he was a professor in the Materials Science and Engineering Department at Suzuka National College of Technology in Japan. He also expressed concern about the education system in Japan and wanted to improve it. He suggested that we collaborate on education projects to benefit students in the United States and Japan. Of course, I was very happy and honored by this offer. We continued to exchange ideas and email messages throughout the year. In 2002, I was invited to serve as a Visiting Professor at Suzuka National College of Technology (SNCT). I returned to Japan as a Visiting Professor in 2005 and as a Keynote Speaker and Visiting Professor in 2008.

CHAPTER 6

Creative Education

International Program

Professor Kanematsu of Japan and I are carrying out an international program in Creative Education. This successful project has already received national awards from the American Chemical Society (ACS) in 2004 and 2007. Major program goals are to turn students of all ages onto science and engineering and to prepare them to be critical thinkers and creative problem solvers. In order to survive in our ever-changing world, the younger generation (our future leaders, scientists, and engineers) must be able to solve new and challenging problems. The Creative Education program is being presented through workshops in the United States and Japan. Malaysia and Korea are also interested in this project, which has five main components.

Program Components

1. *Multisensory Teaching Approach:* This method, also known as the Chemical Sensation Project, takes advantage of students' senses. It is designed to meet individuals' needs and requires teachers to incorporate visual, writing, listening, and laboratory activities into

their science lessons. I prepared special materials for this component and Kanematsu translated them into Japanese. The items include a music CD of science songs, overhead transparencies, pictures to serve as visual aids, hands-on science experiments, science questions, and evaluation forms. Students begin each multisensory lesson by viewing the activity picture and words to the selected science song, while listening to the song. Next they perform an exciting science experiment that complements the song. Finally they answer activity questions and complete the evaluation forms. One lesson is about chemicals. Keep in mind that everything is made of chemicals. Students begin by viewing a picture of table salt (sodium chloride), while listening to the song "Chemicals" on the music CD, *Chemical Sensation with the Barry Tones* (8). Then they carry out a complementary science activity. The students analyze and determine the physical properties (such as color, size, and shape) of common household items like table salt, flour, sugar, apples and oranges.

2. *Science Fair Project Teaching Approach:* This method gives students an opportunity to select an interesting problem to solve for their science fair project. They develop problem-solving and critical thinking skills by performing mental exercises in collecting, analyzing, and interpreting data to draw conclusions about the outcome of their exciting investigations. In addition they prepare creative posters and displays of their work. Science fairs are relatively new in Japan. Therefore Kanematsu and I prepared a book written in Japanese for the Japanese students. It

is titled *Science Fair Fun in Japan* and was published in 2005 by Gendai Tosho, Japan. I also coauthored a similar book written in English, *Plan, Develop, Display, Present Science Projects* published in 2008 by Teacher Created Resources, California.

3. *Reading and Solving a Mystery Teaching Approach:* This innovative method provides students with an opportunity to develop critical thinking and creative problem-solving skills by reading stories and solving a mystery. This technique can be used with any mystery. However to complement our program, Kanematsu and I published creative science books in 2007 (9). These books include a problem-solving model, two short stories, and a detailed science education component. Students master the steps of a problem-solving model by acting as detectives to analyze the short stories and solve their crimes (problems).

4. *Space Science Teaching Approach:* Using space-related activities is a great way to learn science. Middle school, high school and college students in the United States, Malaysia, and Japan are actively participating in this exciting portion of the Creative Education program. They are learning about space exploration, the planets, mission positions and duties, instrumentation, and a teamwork approach to solving problems. Program activities include planet and star gazing, planetarium shows, rocket launching, data analysis, and space-related missions and simulations.

5. *Creative Engineering Design Teaching Approach:* This method combines creative science and engineering design. It is intended to help individuals

meet the needs and challenges of the future. Some activities performed by the participants include creating tasty treats, colorful artwork, and imaginary planets. They also designed boats made of various materials to carry cargo and models of rovers to be used for exploring the surface of Mars.

In addition, Dr. Kanematsu and I successfully carried out NASA's (National Aeronautic and Space Administration's) lunar greenhouse challenge with students in the United States and Japan in 2008. The participants designed, built, and tested greenhouses for growing plants on the surface of the Moon. This is important because man would like to be able to grow plants to supplement meals and produce oxygen for long duration missions to the Moon. The U.S. students used their lunar greenhouses to compare the growth of cinnamon basil seeds flown on the Space Shuttle Endeavor (STS -118 Mission) to Earth-based seeds.

I feel that God wants me to collaborate with Professor Kanematsu by promoting creative thinking at the international level. This is very important in terms of human existence. In order to survive, individuals must be able to creatively solve the new and challenging problems of our ever-changing world.

CHAPTER 7

Church Music

The Trumpet

The Church considers music to be very important and has used it for hundreds of years. Since about the seventh century, the basic vocal music of the Church has been Gregorian Chant, named in honor of Pope St. Gregory the Great. Today music and songs are used for the entrance, the Mass parts, the Offertory, the Communion, and at the end of the service. Music is especially valued during Holy Day celebrations like Christmas and Easter.

When I was nine years old, I learned to play the trumpet. My musically talented father agreed to give me lessons before they were available at school, because I was able to make sounds the first time I blew into the horn.

I have played the trumpet and have sung in choirs for many years. I still perform in bands, brass groups, and ensembles for special celebration Masses at St. Mary's Church in Canton. Also I sing in St. Mary's choir.

I love music and am very proud to play the trumpet, an instrument that is mentioned in the Bible and in the verses of Church songs. The Bible's Exodus section called The Fear of God, includes a trumpet. It mentions that when the people witnessed the thunder and lightning, the trumpet blast, and the mountain smoking, they all feared and trembled. Then they moved to a location farther away (Exodus 20:18).

The Book of Revelation introduces seven trumpets and describes the purpose of each one.

"The seven angels who minister in God's presence were given seven trumpets" (Revelation 8:2).

When the seventh angel blew his trumpet, loud voices in heaven cried out. "The Kingdom of the world now belongs to our Lord and to his Anointed One, and He shall reign forever and ever" (Revelation 11:15).

The sound of the last trumpet is truly a wonderful moment. "The trumpet will sound and the dead will be raised incorruptible, and we shall be changed" (1 Corinthians 15:52).

The trumpet is also used for Church song lyrics. The first verse of *Let Us Go to the Altar* (10) starts with the following phrase. "Give praise with blast of trumpet."

The third verse of *Mine Eyes Have Seen the Glory* (11) includes the following sentence. "He has sounded forth the trumpet that shall never call retreat."

The concluding words of Dan Schutte's song, *Sing a New Song*, are the following (12). "The trumpet sounds, the dead shall be raised. I know my Savior lives."

Healing Mass

The extra-special feeling that I have about music came to me at a healing Mass in 1995. I recall this event very well. It was exciting to be a member of the choir for a special healing Mass held at St. Mary's Church in Canton. Jeanine Nichols was the famous healer who led the service, which had a very peaceful and relaxing atmosphere. I am astonished to say that her three hour service of tranquility seemed like only ten minutes in length. The time rapidly disappeared. She stood on the altar (in the front of the Church) praying, meditating, and speaking. She described certain ailments and diseases. Then individuals having these conditions came forward. When Jeanine laid hands on them, many collapsed. They were slain in the Spirit. This literally means to lose control over one's body and fall to the ground. However no one actually fell to the floor, because they were caught in advance by volunteers. It was a fascinating experience to witness people being healed and slain in the Spirit by God.

To my amazement, in the middle of this extraordinary service, Jeanine Nichols quickly descended the altar steps and rushed over to the choir. She put her left arm around Carolyn Shelmidine and her right arm around me. Then she prayed over us saying that we would be musicians of the Church for God. Ever since that night I have had a very special feeling in my heart. I believe that whenever I sing or play the trumpet at Church, I am really performing for God.

CHAPTER 8

Monsignor Service

Turkey Dinner

In 1996, Monsignor Gerald Service came to St. Mary's in Canton to begin his term as pastor. He was a good manager of money and was able to quickly change the financial situation of the Parish from that of accumulating debt to one which had no debt. Monsignor Service felt a strong commitment to serving the poor, so he established a St. Vincent de Paul clothing store in a house owned by the church. Also he set up a food bank in the church. Since I was an active member of the church and choir, I grew to know and respect him, both as a priest and as a true servant of God.

During the Ice Storm of 1998, many people in Northern New York and Canada were stranded and without electric power for a week or more. Monsignor Service used resources available at St. Mary's School for a major effort to help the Canton Community recover. The school (after receiving a large generator from the National Guard) served as a shelter and provided more than 8000 meals, many of which were prepared by Monsignor himself. He was a kind, caring, and thoughtful person who literally lived up to his name (Service).

Monsignor loved to cook and always looked forward to helping prepare St. Mary's annual turkey dinner. This delicious feast (of baked turkey, gravy, squash, mashed potatoes, vegetables, desserts, and all the trimmings) was a great fundraiser that attracted hundreds of people.

In October of 2002, even though he had health issues with his heart and knees, Monsignor was very excited about the upcoming turkey dinner. I recall talking to him after Mass, just one week before his knee surgery. He seemed confident about the operation and thought that he would heal quickly and feel okay when the dinner date arrived in November. Monsignor also told me that his knees had been bothering him for a long time, so he hoped the surgery would reduce the pain and improve his ability to walk.

Monsignor's knee operation took place at the Ogdensburg hospital and seemed to be successful. However, a blood clot soon formed and caused complications. He was then rushed to a hospital in Burlington, Vermont, where he died after a short stay. Our congregation and the local community were saddened and shocked by his sudden and unexpected death.

St. Mary's Parish celebrated Monsignor's life and contributions to society in a very wonderful funeral Mass led by Father Timothy Canaan, who took over as Pastor until 2008. During his homily, Father Canaan emphasized the importance of the turkey dinner to Monsignor Service and encouraged the Parish to prepare and serve this special meal in memory of Monsignor.

The music for this Mass was beautiful, so I was proud to be a member of the choir. While sitting with the musicians in the balcony, I scanned the crowded Church and noticed many people crying, wiping away tears, and blowing their noses. I felt very odd and out of place, because I had a happy feeling in my heart. My body was overwhelmed with joy. I believed that Monsignor was at peace and with God.

More than twenty years had passed, since I promised to say a daily rosary. By 2002 I had already said thousands of them. I prayed rosaries at home, in Church, and while taking a walk. On November 6, 2002 (a few days before Monsignor's Memorial Dinner), I was saying a rosary for Monsignor during my late night stroll. Even though the rectory was dark and empty, I momentarily stood in front of it thinking. I was wondering if Monsignor's spirit would be present for the special turkey dinner held in his honor. At that moment, I unintentionally said Monsignor Service's name out loud. Immediately, a giant wall of white light appeared, with a white nondescript pulsating figure in its center. The figure's movement reminded me of a large white beating heart. I was in a state of shock and could not believe my eyes. This huge wall, above the rectory's front entrance, completely covered the second level. The spectacular vision appeared and disappeared five times in a row. I was convinced that Monsignor had communicated with me.

Dana Barry

Canton Rectory with Large Wall of Light

(Sketch by Dana Barry)

CHAPTER 9

Blessed Mother

Peaceful Dream

In September of 2003 (after saying daily rosaries for 24 years), I felt that my prayers needed to be stronger and more powerful. Each night during the months of September and October, I prayed that God, the Blessed Mother, and my Guardian Angel would be with me at all times to provide guidance and protection.

During the night of October 7, 2003, I had the most wonderful and peaceful dream ever. The setting was an immense beautiful garden of colorful and fragrant flowers with lovely singing birds and fluorescent butterflies. It was surrounded by grass and trees of various bright shades of green and by natural pools of sparkling blue water. While walking alone in this tranquil paradise, I saw many large white angels fly past me and a huge pink crucifix in the sky. (Refer to the front cover of this book.) My body was completely relaxed and at peace. I was so overwhelmed with joy and happiness that I wanted to remain there forever.

The morning of October 8 arrived and I woke up as usual. However, I still felt very elated, relaxed, and wonderful. It was truly the best feeling that I have ever experienced.

Beautiful Lady

Little did I know that my greatest surprise was yet to come. On October 19, 2003, I crawled into bed several hours after my husband retired for the night. Upon closing my eyes, I saw two white angels with gold trumpets float in front of me, as if they were leading a procession to the right side of the room. Then they disappeared. Completely puzzled by this vision, I immediately rolled from my back onto my left side and faced the wall. What I saw was unbelievable. Standing in front of me was an enormous beautiful lady embedded in thousands of small white lights. Her eyes and hair were both light brown, but her skin and smiling face were as white as chalk. She was completely dressed in various shades of white and appeared to be made of light. I didn't know who she was until my eyes focused on her chest, which exposed many large brown thorns. Instantaneously I grabbed for Her outstretched hand, but the Blessed Mother disappeared.

This blessed event was a complete shock to my body. My heart was beating rapidly and I was panting and gasping for air. I made such a commotion that my husband yelled out, "Dana, what's the matter with you? Are you okay?" I briefly told him what happened and then we both went to sleep.

I feel that the Blessed Mother appeared to me as an answer to my prayers. I truly believe that She is with me at all times.

The Blessed Mother Embedded in Lights

(Sketch by Dana Barry)

CHAPTER 10

Not Alone

Shared Experiences

It is true that I have had some unique spiritual experiences. However, I am not alone. Over the years I have read books about this topic and discussed it with people of various backgrounds and religions. I found many examples of extraordinary events. A few are described using fictitious names to maintain confidentiality.

A priest at St. Mary's Parish shared a special story with the congregation. He told us the real reason why he became a priest. While growing up his dream was to become a lawyer, get married, raise a family, and own a nice house with a double garage and a pool. He also had an inner feeling that maybe he should become a priest. Even though he had a steady girlfriend and other options, he joined the seminary to solve this dilemma. After a short stay, he was planning to quit. During this time period, he did volunteer work in a soup kitchen for the homeless to boost up his resume. While serving soup to an older man with grey hair and a beard, he heard

God's voice say "The Body of Christ!" At that moment he decided to become a priest.

Lou told me that while repairing his ceiling, a large section of it fell but missed him. He believes that an angel made the pieces fall to the left instead of directly on top of him.

June said that while driving to the hospital to visit a sick friend, she saw a ball of bright white light rise from the ground into the sky. Upon arriving at the hospital, she found out that her good friend had just died. She believes that the ball of white light was his spirit.

Ann was very ill while driving a car. Before becoming unconscious, she recalls foreseeing a head on collision with a large truck. When she woke up, her car was parked safely on the edge of the road. She believes that an angel or spirit drove the car for her.

Jack was saying a rosary while driving late at night on a secluded road. After saying the following words aloud, "This rosary is for my Guardian Angel," his car was completely encapsulated in a bright white light.

While receiving Communion at church, Paula vividly saw a Crown of Thorns on the Host.

A lady at St. Mary's Parish had such a bad case of crippling arthritis that her husband carried her into church each Sunday. After attending a healing Mass, she was able to walk again.

One of my friends (who prays a lot) had her rosary turn gold. I had an opportunity to see the rosary before and after it turned gold.

Cherie was troubled with many problems, so she prayed to her angel. Finally one night a white light in the shape of a lady appeared in her bedroom. Cherie believes that the apparition was an angel responding to her prayers.

I recall a last visit with my 91-year-old friend Lea. She was always so very kind, helpful, and compassionate to others, that I thought of her as a wonderful missionary. Even though she was dying, our final visit seemed joyful. Lea appeared happy and told me that her room was full of angels who would soon take her to Heaven.

Spiritual Reading

On October 2, 1932, Saint Therese appeared in the Chapel of St. Mary's Convent in Canton, New York. This special event is described in a book about St. Mary's

Parish (13). Sister Mary Aloysia (who taught first and second graders at St. Mary's School) was devoted to Saint Therese and asked her for a sign. In the early morning of October 2, a first grader named Francis Doyle brought Sister Aloysia a beautiful yellow rose with tinges of pink in it. He told her that his mother bought the flower and wanted it placed on the altar. Sister granted the request and placed it there before going to school. That evening she summoned the other nuns to the Chapel and told them to look toward the altar. To their greatest surprise, they saw Saint Therese as a small child in a First Communion dress resting against the petals of the rose.

The Blessed Mother makes appearances throughout the world. She works in collaboration with Her Son and has an important role in the lives of the faithful on Earth. Saints who have seen Her include Saint Gertrude, Saint Francis of Assisi, Saint Bridget of Sweden, Saint Catherine of Siena, and others. In the Asia Minor town of Neocaesarea during the third century after Christ, Gregory (today known as St. Gregory, the Wonder-worker) heard that he was to be ordained a priest by the archbishop. At this time there was much controversy over the nature of the Holy Trinity. Gregory was so troubled by this problem, that before agreeing to become a priest he fled to the desert seeking God's help through prayer. To his amazement St. John (John the Evangelist) and the Blessed Mother appeared to him in a dream, where he was told that the Father has never been without the Son and the Son has never been without the Spirit (14).

The Blessed Mother has also appeared to other people including the children Francesco, Jacinta, and Lucia in Fatima, Portugal during the year 1917 and to Sister Agnes Sasagawa of Akita, Japan in 1973 (15).

CHAPTER 11

The Answer

Religious Puzzle

I have been puzzled by my spiritual experiences for thirty years. Even though I continue to say daily rosaries, I haven't spent much time reading the Bible and other religious books. Therefore, I have never really understood the extraordinary events taking place in my life. Fortunately I keep a spiritual diary, which means I record the date, some information, and a sketch for each experience.

In 2008, I tried to solve this religious puzzle by using my Creative Problem-Solving Model (16). My problem to be solved is written as the following question. What is the meaning of my spiritual experiences?

Creative Problem-Solving Model

1. *Problem:* That which needs to be solved (answered).

2. *Available Information:* This is available data that relates to the problem.

3. *Other Needed Data:* This is other required information needed to solve the problem.

4. *Procedure to Obtain Needed Data:* A method should be prepared to obtain data needed for solving the problem.

5. *Record the Data:* All information pertaining to the problem should be recorded.

6. *Organize the Data:* Organize the information in a logical and useful way. (For example, list events in chronological order.)

7. *Analyze the Data:* Closely study all of the information.

8. *Generalize from the Data:* Use the information to make some general statements.

9. *Decision Making:* Make a decision that hopefully solves the problem (answers the question).

The following is a detailed description of my spiritual investigation using the Creative Problem-Solving Model.

1. *Problem:* What is the meaning of my spiritual experiences?

2. *Available Information:* This information is listed in chronological order.

   • July 1979: I started to pray rosaries asking God for a sign to strengthen my faith.

   • Late October 1979: An apparition made of light appeared next to the wall phone in my kitchen. It was sky blue in color and shaped like a human. However, it had a head that looked like the yellow Sun. After encountering this vision, I promised God that I would say a rosary everyday until I die.

- November 6, 2002: While taking an evening walk, I was saying a rosary for Monsignor Service so that his soul would go to Heaven. When I unintentionally said his name out loud (in front of the dark, empty rectory), a giant wall of white light appeared with a white nondescript pulsating figure in its center. It completely covered the second level of the rectory's front entrance. This spectacular vision appeared and disappeared five times in a row.

- September 2003: I wanted my prayers to be stronger and more powerful so each night I asked God, the Blessed Mother, and my Guardian Angel to be with me at all times to provide guidance and protection.

- October 7, 2003: I had the most wonderful dream and relaxed feeling ever. I was in a garden of paradise. It was very peaceful with beautiful birds, flowers and fluorescent butterflies. It also had natural pools of sparkling blue water surrounded by bright green grass and trees. Many large white angels were flying around me and a huge pink crucifix appeared in the sky. I wanted to stay there forever, but awoke the morning of October 8 still feeling very elated and relaxed.

- October 19, 2003: Upon closing my eyes in bed, I saw two white angels with gold trumpets float in front of me. Then I saw an enormous lady, embedded in thousands of white lights. She had light brown eyes and light brown hair, but her smiling face and skin were as white as chalk.

She was completely dressed in various shades of white and appeared to be made of light. Her left hand was extended to me. I didn't know who she was until my eyes focused on her chest, which exposed many large brown thorns. She was the Blessed Mother.

3. *Other Needed Data:* Other information needed to help solve this problem is to know the meaning of the Sun and brown thorns and the importance of the occurrence dates and colors of the visions.

4. *Procedure to Obtain Needed Data:*
   - Pray for guidance and knowledge
   - Talk to priests and close friends
   - Read the Bible and other religious books

5. *Record the New Data:*
   - Dates
     - October is the month of the rosary.
     - October 7 is devoted to Our Lady of the Rosary.
     - November is the month of All Souls.
   - Colors
     - Yellow is the color of the Sun.
     - White signifies purity. Saints like Saint Bridget of Sweden saw the Blessed Mother wearing shiny white clothes (17). White and white light are often associated with angels.
     - Blue (actually sky blue) is considered to be the color of Our Lady's mantle or cloak (18), especially for Our Lady of Graces or as The Immaculate Conception.

- The Sun
  - An image resembling the Sun is displayed in the chest area of the Blessed Mother on my thirty-year-old Brown Scapular. This Scapular, representing the armor and protection of Our Lady, was given to Saint Simon Stock in 1251 with the following promise (19). "Whosoever dies wearing this Scapular shall not suffer eternal fire."
  - On October 13, 1917, Our Lady was responsible for the Miracle of the Sun that took place in front of at least 50,000 people in Fatima, Portugal (20).
  - The Sun is mentioned in the Bible (Matthew 17:2) section called Jesus Transfigured. "He was transfigured before their eyes. His face became as dazzling as the Sun, etc."
- The Thorns
  - Our Lady of Sorrows has seven thorns in Her chest. Each thorn represents a specific Sorrow. The Seven Sorrows are listed below.

  1. The prophecy of Simeon (He alluded to the suffering of Jesus.)
  2. The flight into Egypt
  3. The loss of the Holy Child Jesus in the Temple
  4. The meeting of Jesus and Mary on the Way of the Cross
  5. The death of Jesus
  6. The piercing of the side of Jesus and the taking down of His body from the Cross
  7. The burial of Jesus

- Around the year 1346, the Blessed Mother told Bridget (St. Bridget of Sweden) to meditate on Her sorrows and tears (21). The Novena prayers for our Lady of Sorrows were passed to us by this saint. Previously in 1239 the Blessed Mother appeared to the Seven Servite Fathers from Florence, Italy. She presented them with a black habit to wear as a reminder of the sorrows She experienced through Her Son's crucifixion and death. These men laid down the foundation for the Order of Servants of Mary, a group which spread devotion to the Sorrowful Virgin Mother (22).

6. *Organize the Data:* All of the information is displayed on an organized chart titled Spiritual Events. See page 51.

7. *Analyze the Data:* The information is studied and analyzed.

8. *Generalize from the Data:* General statements are made.

   - For each spiritual experience, I had been praying for a special request. My prayers were heard and answered with a vision. I believe that the vision in November was intended to confirm my inner feeling that Monsignor's Soul was with God.

   - The other three spectacular events took place in October (the month of the Rosary). Therefore I feel that they all involve the Blessed Mother. It is possible that the 1979 spirit symbolizes the Blessed Mother. The sky blue color could

SPIRITUAL EVENTS

Date	Importance of Date	Prayer Request	Vision	Other Information
Late October 1979	Month of the Rosary	For a Sign from God	A human-shaped spirit made of light appeared next to the wall phone in my kitchen. It was sky blue in color with a yellow Sun for its head. Sky blue is considered to be the color of Our Lady's mantle or cloak.	Our Lady is responsible for the Miracle of the Sun. Also an image resembling the Sun is on my 30-year-old Brown Scapular. Matthew 17:2 (Jesus Transfigured. "His face became as dazzling as the Sun.") After this vision, I promised to say a daily rosary until I die.
Nov. 6, 2002	Month of All Souls	For Monsignor Service's Soul to go to Heaven	A giant wall of white light with a white nondescript pulsating figure in its center appeared at the Canton rectory. The vision appeared and disappeared five times in a row. It covered the outside of the rectory's second level, above the front entrance.	When I mentioned Monsignor's name out loud (while praying for him in front of the rectory), the vision immediately appeared.
Oct. 7, 2003	Day Devoted to Our Lady of the Rosary	For God, the Blessed Mother, and my Guardian Angel to be with me at all times	Through a dream, I was in a very peaceful and wonderful garden of paradise with beautiful and colorful flowers, birds, etc. It had many large white angels flying around me and a huge pink crucifix in the sky.	I wanted to stay in the garden forever, because it was the best feeling I have ever had. When I awoke on October 8, I still felt very elated and relaxed.
Oct. 19, 2003	Month of the Rosary	For God, the Blessed Mother, and my Guardian Angel to be with me at all times	In my bedroom appeared two white angels with gold trumpets, followed by Our Lady of Sorrows. Her chest exposed large brown thorns. Each thorn represents a specific Sorrow. She was enormous and embedded in thousands of white lights.	The Blessed Mother had light brown eyes, light brown hair, a smiling face, and Her skin was as white as chalk. She was completely dressed in various shades of white and appeared to be made of light. Her left hand was extended to me.

represent her cloak and the yellow Sun could relate to Her Miracle of the Sun. My wonderful experience in the perfect garden of paradise took place on October 7, the Day devoted to Our Lady of the Rosary. Also my greatest and most treasured surprise was the Blessed Mother's visit on October 19, 2003. She was smiling, but appeared as Our Lady of Sorrows with large thorns in Her chest. I believe that the Blessed Mother is pleased with my daily rosaries. However, She also wants me to know about Her Sorrows.

9. *Decision Making:* The answer to my question is provided.

- Question: What is the meaning of my spiritual experiences?

- Answer: I believe that my spiritual experiences confirm that God does indeed hear and answer our prayers. Also I feel that the Blessed Mother is with me on my journey of life.

CHAPTER 12
Journey Continues

God's Plan

This book was mainly written in October, the month of the rosary. It has allowed me to express and share my extraordinary religious experiences. Each event, including the book itself, was God's answer to a particular set of prayers and requests. I believe that God has a special plan for each of us.

Mother Teresa (of Calcutta) was born in 1910 as Agnes Bojaxhiu in Macedonia, the former Yugoslavia. As a teenager she was very involved in activities at her local parish. At age 17 she responded to her first call (from God) to serve as a Catholic Missionary nun. When she took her vows as a Sister of Loretto, an Order working in India, Agnes selected the name Teresa. Later in 1944 she became sick with tuberculosis. While riding in a train to Darjeeling, the place where she would recuperate from this illness, Sister Teresa received her second call. She was to leave the convent and work with the poor while living among them (23).

In 1216, Brother Francis (St. Francis of Assisi) who had previously been a worldly person and a playboy, devotedly and persistently prayed for the Lord's forgiveness of his sins. He heard Christ's voice say that his sins were removed. Brother Francis was so very grateful that it was his passionate desire and new purpose in life to obtain the same favor for all repentant sinners. After many intense prayers Jesus and the Blessed Mother appeared to him and granted this request, which became known as the Portiuncula (Little Portion) Indulgence. It provided an opportunity for certain individuals (those who have confessed their sins, have been absolved from the sins, and who are truly sorry for committing them) to receive complete forgiveness both in this world and the next by entering the chapel of Our Lady of the Angels, which was also called the Little Portion or Portiuncula (24).

As a result of saying many prayers and reflecting upon my life, I feel that my main purpose is threefold:

1. To pray for everyone (the sick, the poor, those suffering in any way, the priests, etc.), for all Souls, and for good causes such as world peace.

2. To assist Dr. Roger Haw, Ansted University and others in their efforts to pursue world peace by promoting the practice of social responsibility.

3. To collaborate with Dr. Hideyuki Kanematsu and others by promoting creative thinking globally, so that future generations will be able to creatively solve new and challenging problems.

This book was inspired by God and written to help others recognize, appreciate, and pursue the special plans that God has for them.

God Listens

I am imperfect and have many flaws. However, I have learned a lot and matured spiritually over the years. We are all on a journey and must carry our crosses of suffering and pain. Eventually, we will die just as Jesus Christ did. Hopefully we are selected to rejoice with Him in Heaven.

God is willing to help us with our daily struggles and challenges of life. All we need to do is ask. He listens to our prayers and answers them in His own time and in a way that is best for us. It is never too late to seek God's assistance. He is always there and ready to help all of us: the rich; the poor; religious leaders; lay people; and those living in large cities, small towns, and various countries throughout the world.

I believe that prayers are powerful and can be used to promote world peace and to unite our global community. Life on Earth could be more like Heaven if each individual, especially our global leaders, would pray for this goal and treat others with kindness and respect.

REFERENCES

1. Brown, Raphael. *Saints Who Saw Mary*. Rockford, Illinois: Tan Books and Publishers, Inc. 101 (1994).

2. http://www.ewtn.com/motherteresa/words.htm

3. De Montfort, St. Louis (translated by Mary Barbour). *The Secret of the Rosary*. New York: Montfort Publications (1954).

4. Johnson, Kevin Orlin. *Why Do Catholics Do That?* New York: Ballantine Publishing, 96 (1994).

5. Barry, Dana M. "Hazard Communication and Training: A Prototype," *Journal of Environmental Health*, **50**, 18 (July/August 1987).

6. Barry, Dana M. "Chem-Is-Tree," *Journal of Chemical Education*, **74**, 1175 (1997).

7. Barry, Dana M. "The Environmental Risks of Using Combustion as a Source of Energy," *American Chemical Society's On-Line CONFCHEM* (2001).

8. Barry, Dana M. (copyright holder of CD) *Chemical Sensation with the Barry Tones* (1996).

9. Barry, Dana M. and Kanematsu, Hideyuki. *Develop Critical Thinking Skills, Solve a Mystery, Learn Science*. Oklahoma: Tate Publishing (2007). The authors' Japanese edition of this book is published by Pleiades of Japan (2007).

10. Schutte, Daniel. "Let Us Go to the Altar," *Today's Missal/Music Issue*. Portland, Oregon: OCP Publishing (2007).

11. Ibid. "Mine Eyes Have Seen the Glory."

12. Ibid. "Sing a New Song."

13. Ames, Lawrence, Barry, Brian, Carson, Patricia, Finnegan, Eugene, Livernois, Sandy, Martin, Dorajean, Mintener, Marilyn, Krenceski, Irene, O'Horo, Cathy, Richards, Debbie, Smith, Margaret, and Sweeney, Dan. *History of Canton's St. Mary's Parish 1874-1999*, 23 (1999).

14. Brown, Raphael. *Saints Who Saw Mary*. Rockford, Illinois: Tan Books and Publishers, Inc., 3 (1994).

15. Flynn, Ted and Maureen. *The Warning, The Miracle, The Chastisement, The Era of Peace*. U.S.: MaxKol Communications, Inc., 181 (1993).

16. Barry, Dana M. and Kanematsu, Hideyuki. *Develop Critical Thinking Skills, Solve a Mystery, Learn Science*. Oklahoma: Tate Publishing, 103 (2007).

17. Brown, Raphael. *Saints Who Saw Mary*. Rockford, Illinois: Tan Books and Publishers, Inc. 61 (1994).

18. Johnson, Kevin Orlin. *Why Do Catholics Do That?* New York: Ballantine Publishing, 237 (1994).

19. Brown, Raphael. *Saints Who Saw Mary*. Rockford, Illinois: Tan Books and Publishers, Inc. 41 (1994).

20. Flynn, Ted and Maureen. *The Warning, The Miracle, The Chastisement, The Era of Peace*. U.S.: MaxKol Communications, Inc., 137 (1993).

21. Brown, Raphael. *Saints Who Saw Mary*. Rockford, Illinois: Tan Books and Publishers, Inc. 64 (1994).

22. Ibid. page 40.

23. http://www.ewtn.com/motherteresa/life.htm

24. Brown, Raphael. *Saints Who Saw Mary*. Rockford, Illinois: Tan Books and Publishers, Inc. 26 (1994).

ABOUT THE AUTHOR

Dr. Dana M. Barry is the Senior Technical Writer and Editor at Clarkson University's Center for Advanced Materials Processing (CAMP). She is a Certified Professional Chemist, Scientific Board President for Ansted University, and an officer for the Northern New York section of the American Chemical Society (ACS). Dr. Barry organized three World First Space Missions and served as a Visiting Professor in Malaysia (2001, 2004, and 2007), England (2003), and Japan (2002, 2005, and 2008). During her 2008 visit to Japan, she gave the Keynote Address ("Turning Children onto Science") at Suzuka City's Education Symposium. Dr. Barry has more than 150 professional publications including eleven books. She also has numerous honors and awards, including national awards from the American Chemical Society and fourteen consecutive APEX Awards for Publication Excellence (1996–2009). In addition, she is a member of St. Mary's Parish in Canton, New York, and loves to sing, pray, and play the trumpet.

Breinigsville, PA USA
19 November 2009
227885BV00001B/72/P